COOL

BOOK

Marianne Murphy

For Ellen and Tom

RULES FOR YOUR COOL BOOK

1. Spelling doesn't matter

2. Grammar doesn't matter

3. Nothing matters

4. You can write on the pages

5. It doesn't have to be good

6. You don't have to go in order

7. You don't have to share it

8. You don't have to do anything

9. Rules are nothing

10. You're free

TABLE OF CONTENTS
(arranged by prompt type)

ONE WORD PROMPTS

Let each word inspire whatever

stories, poems, rants, raves, rambles,

dialogues, scripts, pictures, photos,

maps, puzzles, recipes, lyrics . . .

anything that comes to mind.

Word: Alchemy

Word: Pirate

Word: Invisible

Word: Nautical

Word: Prism

Word: Bubble

Word: Eyeglasses

Word: Constellation

Word: Chimes

Word: Village

Word: Rollercoaster

Word: Seaside

Word: Jacket

Word: Snowman

Word: Death

BIOGRPAHY PROMPTS

These are questions about your life and preferences. You do not need to answer them directly. You do not need to be honest. You do not need to answer as yourself. You do not need to answer in words. You do not need to answer at all.

What is the most important
thing you own?

What job would you hate to have, even for a week?

What's the most impressive
thing you know how to do?

What would the perfect version
of you be like?

What would you do if you had to spend a million dollars in a single day?

What unsettles you the most?

If someone painted a portrait of you, how would you want it to look?

What part of your life do you think would make a good movie?

What's the coolest thing
someone you know has said?

What is something you think
people take too seriously?

What do you think changed you
the most?

What's something you want to change but know you can't?

What are three skills you would like to immediately acquire?

Who is your favorite historical figure and why?

What are you running from?

FICTION PROMPTS

These are prompts to make

something up. It can be in any form

or medium you want. It can be

complete fiction. It can be heavily

based on your life with only the

names changed. It can be anything.

Write about two people seeing
each other for the first time.

Write something inspired by a
dream you had recently.

Write about someone who is eavesdropping.

Write about an unusual
addiction or obsession.

Write something that takes place entirely while someone is doing the dishes.

Write something really, really, really boring.

Write the shopping list of an
unusual creature.

Rewrite the first paragraph of any book, with your own words and details.

Write something that takes
place during a camping trip.

Write about someone who is
choosing not to speak.

Write something where the last line is a very common punch-line.

Write something that starts at
sunrise and ends at sunset.

Write something where two characters are handcuffed together.

Write something that takes place in the ten seconds before someone wakes up.

Write something that is also
secretly a recipe.

LIST PROMPTS

These are lists. Lists can help you get

focused, or they can help your mind

wander. You do not need to fill them

out as yourself. No rules.

Make a list of your favorite songs.

1.

2.

3.

4.

5.

6.

7.

8.

9.

10.

Make a list of your favorite
scenes from movies.

1.

2.

3.

4.

5.

6.

7.

8.

9.

10.

Make a list of your favorite books.

1.

2.

3.

4.

5.

6.

7.

8.

9.

10.

Make a list of things you want
to see.

1.

2.

3.

4.

5.

6.

7.

8.

9.

10.

Make a list of times you
laughed really hard.

1.

2.

3.

4.

5.

6.

7.

8.

9.

10.

Make a list of times you cried.

1.

2.

3.

4.

5.

6.

7.

8.

9.

10.

Make a list of places you want
to go.

1.

2.

3.

4.

5.

6.

7.

8.

9.

10.

Make a list of names you like.

1.

2.

3.

4.

5.

6.

7.

8.

9.

10.

Make a list of imaginary words.

1.

2.

3.

4.

5.

6.

7.

8.

9.

10.

Make a list of the worst things
you can think of.

1.

2.

3.

4.

5.

6.

7.

8.

9.

10.

Make a list of things you're
afraid of.

1.

2.

3.

4.

5.

6.

7.

8.

9.

10.

Make a list of things you wish
people knew about you.

1.

2.

3.

4.

5.

6.

7.

8.

9.

10.

Make a list of sensations you love.

1.

2.

3.

4.

5.

6.

7.

8.

9.

10.

Make a list of your favorite
words.

1.

2.

3.

4.

5.

6.

7.

8.

9.

10.

Make a list of your favorite sounds.

1.

2.

3.

4.

5.

6.

7.

8.

9.

10.

CHARACTER PROMPTS

Make up some characters, or alter

ones you already have. You don't

have to introduce them. These can

be stories, poems, fragments, lists,

lyrics, scribbles, photos, drawings . . .

anything that captures your

characters the way you want.

Make up a character who is a giant.

Make up a character you hate.

Make up a character who is the opposite of you.

Make up a character who is
exactly the same as you.

Make up a character who can't
die.

Make up a character who has never been outside.

Make up a character who is
dreaming.

Make up a character who was
just born.

Make up a character who keeps
repeating the same day.

Make up a character who can't cook.

Make up a character who did something terrible.

Make up a character who has never done anything wrong.

Make up a character who lives inside a utensil drawer.

Make up a character who has
no shadow.

Make up a character who
reminds you of someone you've
never met.

PLACE PROMPTS

Let's make up some places. These can be pure fantasy, or based on a place you've been or dreamed about before. You can represent these places however you like. Maybe you can picture them vividly before you start, maybe you can fill them in as you write or draw.

Create a place that's haunted.

Create a place where the sun
has just risen.

Create a place where you feel
safe.

Create a place that reminds
you of a time you were
miserable.

Create a place you'd move to
today if you could.

Create a place that has no
surfaces.

Create a place where no
humans have ever lived.

Create a place where everyone
has your dream job.

Create a place that's the exact
opposite of where you grew up.

Create a place that could've
been included in your favorite
book.

Create a place that you don't
like to think about.

Create a place where
everything is edible.

Create a place that's similar to your favorite planet or celestial body.

Create a place that nobody but
you can find.

Create a place that you're not
allowed to go to.

Time to write some poems! Any form is fine. Haikus, sonnets, limericks, free verse, maybe a form that hasn't even been invented yet . . . you could also try some visual poetry, concrete poetry, or poetry comics. Go for it.

Write a poem about the
weirdest fact you know.

Write a poem about a family
secret.

Write a poem about something
you can see right now.

Write a poem about what it'll
be like outside tonight.

Write a poem about yesterday.

Write an acrostic poem using your favorite name.

Write a poem about something
you can hear right now.

Write a poem which uses your
favorite word six times.

Write a poem that recreates a
memory from your childhood.

Write a poem that portrays a
vision of your future.

Write a poem of questions to a
character you've created.

Write a poem of answers from
that character.

Write an apology poem.

Write a poem about your
favorite season.

Write a poem with your eyes
closed.

DOODLE PROMPTS

Let's draw! Use pencils, colored

pencils, pens, gel pens, crayons,

markers, dirt, stamps, stickers . . . you

can copy other people's drawings,

you can trace. You can even keep

your eyes closed if you want to, or

you can write in the margins if

inspiration strikes.

Draw yourself.

Draw someone near you.

Draw someone you love.

Draw someone you hate.

Draw a monster.

Draw hair.

Draw the ugliest creature in the
world.

Draw a place you want to go.

Draw a place you don't want to
go.

Draw something you wish you
could tape into this book.

Draw what your favorite song
looks like.

Draw a strange Halloween
costume.

Draw what you feel right now.

Draw the best thing you can think of.

Draw the worst thing you can
think of.

SCRAPBOOK PROMPTS

Get some tape or glue or something

adhesive and put some real stuff in

this book! Use whatever feels right.

Printed images, clippings from

magazines, found photos at flea

markets, and old photo albums are

all great places to start.

Attach a picture of yourself here.

Attach a picture of something you love here.

Attach a picture of something
you hate here.

Attach a picture of something you want here.

Attach a picture of your
favorite place here.

Attach a picture here of something that you're drawn to and you don't know why.

Attach a picture of something
that makes you sad here.

Attach a picture of a person
you want to be here.

Attach a picture of something you want to write about here.

Attach a picture of something
you want to learn about here.

Attach a picture of something
you miss here.

Attach a picture of someone
you look up to here.

Attach something you find
outside here.

Attach part of a map here.

Make a collage here.

SONG PROMPTS

Create while you listen to music.

Search for these songs on YouTube

or Spotify and see what comes out if

you try to fill the page while they

play. Any song can be replaced with

a song you like more.

Play "Longest Night" by Alec
Holowka and fill the page.

Play "The Lark Ascending" by
Ralph Vaughan Williams and fill
the page.

Play "Fairy Dance" by James Newton Howard and fill the page.

Play "Sailor" by Hem and fill the
page.

Play "Break My Stride" by
Matthew Wilder and fill the
page.

Play "The Clockwise Witness"
by DeVotchKa and fill the page.

Play "Some Velvet Morning" by
Nancy Sinatra & Lee Hazelwood
and fill the page.

Play "Classical Gas" by Mason Williams and fill the page.

Play "Hey Ya" by OutKast and
fill the page.

Play "Kimberly" by Patti Smith
and fill the page.

Play "Smoke Gets In Your Eyes"
by The Platters and fill the
page.

Play "Summertime" by Clara
Rockmore and fill the page.

Play "Wuthering Heights" by
Kate Bush and fill the page.

Play "Slip" by Elliot Moss and
fill the page.

Play "Little Sadie" by Crooked
Still and fill the page.

LETTER PROMPTS

Now let's write or draw some letters

to real or imaginary recipients. You

don't have to send them. You don't

have to write them as yourself.

You don't have to write them in a

language that exists. They don't

have to be nice.

Write a letter to your best
friend.

Write a letter to your family.

Write a letter to an animal
you've met.

Write a letter to yourself at 5-years-old.

Write a letter to yourself at
90-years-old.

Write a letter to your happiness.

Write a letter to your anger.

Write a letter to your fear.

Write a letter to someone you love.

Write a letter to someone you
hate.

Write a letter to one of your characters.

Write a letter to someone you miss.

Write a letter to your body.

Write a letter to your first
crush.

Write a letter to a ghost.

GOODBYE PROMPT

Fill this with anything else you wish
you could've included in
your cool book.

CPSIA information can be obtained
at www.ICGtesting.com
Printed in the USA
BVHW032019160619
551144BV00001B/3/P

9 780692 146125